Dinosaurs

BY JANE WERNER WATSON

Pictures by
William de J. Rutherfoord

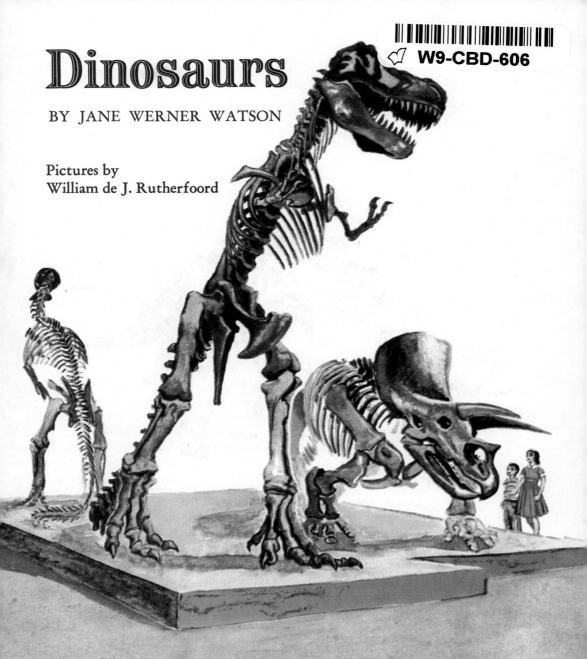

A GOLDEN BOOK • New York
Western Publishing Company, Inc.
Racine, Wisconsin 53404

Few things are more fascinating to a child than the story of the giant creatures that once lived on our earth. Jane Werner Watson's clear, simple text and William de J. Rutherfoord's imaginative illustrations bring to young children a vivid picture of how the world might have been, in the long-ago days of the dinosaurs.

Long, long ago, long before the days of people,
huge creatures called dinosaurs ruled the earth.
We can study only their bones today.
Where did they come from?
Where did they go?
That is the story we wish to know.

In those long-ago days on earth,
the land was sunny and warm and green.
The oceans were full of shelled creatures and fish.
Along the shores in fresh water am-phib-i-ans lived,
young ones in the water, grown-ups on land,
as amphibians do today.

But the only creatures who lived all their lives
on land in those days were reptiles.
Some of these reptiles ate fish.

VARANOPS

Some ate eggs.

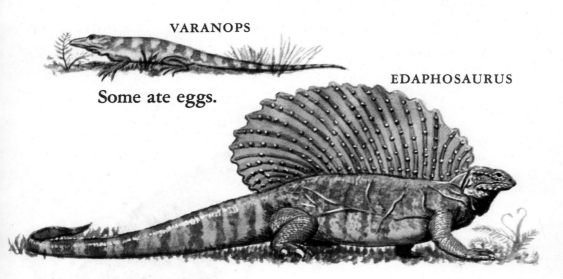

EDAPHOSAURUS

Some ate plants.

PODOKESAURUS

Some ate meat.

There was plenty to eat for all in those days.
So the reptiles grew and GREW and GREW!
Some of them walked on their hind feet.
They grew long, strong hind legs,
and in front they had short, grasping claws.
They shook the earth like thunder when they moved.
They were the dinosaurs.

SALTOPOSUCHUS

COMPSOGNATHUS

Their family name is "saurus," meaning lizard.
They were something like our lizards of today.
"Dino" means terrible,
and some of them were terrible indeed.

ANCHISAURUS

There was Pla-te-o-sau-rus, first of the giants.
He was huge, but not terrible.
He ate green, growing plants.

There was thirty-foot Al-lo-sau-rus.

He ate other dinosaurs.

There was Steg-o-sau-rus, who wore heavy, spiny plates.

There was Bron-to-sau-rus, who was seventy feet long
from the tip of his nose to the tip of his tail.
His tail was so far from his tiny brain
that he had a separate sort of brain back there
to tell his hind legs what to do.

Slow-moving Di-plod-o-cus was sometimes longer still.
They both weighed so much they liked to stand
in swamps where water helped hold up their weight.
They were so big, and they got so hungry, that
they had to munch at green plants all day long.

There was Bra-chi-o-sau-rus, biggest of all.
He weighed as much as fifty tons!
But he couldn't run. He couldn't fight.
When he was frightened, he just hid his head.

The king of giants was Ty-ran-no-sau-rus rex.
A bloodthirsty monster was he. He was fifty feet long.
And his six-inch teeth were sharp as sabers.
He could eat a huge meal.

The other creatures needed protection
to be safe from Ty-ran-no-sau-rus rex and his like.
Some wore coats of armor, covered with spikes and studs.
An-kyl-o-sau-rus was one of these.

Some wore bony helmets with sharp horns.
Tri-cer-a-tops wore one of those.
Some had tails like clubs of bone.
Some had mouths like duck bills,
full of thousands of teeth.

TRACHODON

TRICERATOPS

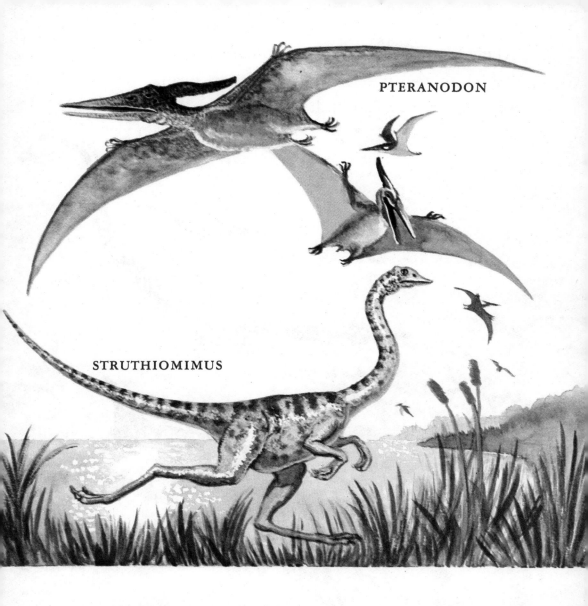

PTERANODON

STRUTHIOMIMUS

Some grew long legs. They learned to run fast.
Ostrich-like Stru-thi-o-mi-mus was one.
Some, like **P-ter-an-o-don**, learned to fly.

Others like Ple-sio-saur and Mo-sa-saur
and Ich-thyo-saur, took to the seas and swam.
Some learned to run and some to swim and some to fly.

PLESIOSAUR

ICHTHYOSAUR

But not one was intelligent.
Their brains were very, very small.
Maybe that was the reason for what happened.

What happened was this.
As the years went by,
all those creatures disappeared.

Giant Bron-to-sau-rus, the thunder lizard,
taller than many trees,
fifty-foot-long Ty-ran-no-sau-rus rex,
bigger than many houses,
and all the rest of them vanished away.

Today the only reptiles that remain
are turtles in their tough and bony shells . . .

small, scaly lizards that live on land
and look like toy dinosaurs . . .

big-jawed, lizard-like crocodiles
and alligators in warm swamps . . .
and long, legless snakes that slither about.

What became of the dinosaurs?
Were the winters too cold or the summers too hot?
Was there not enough food for them?
No one knows for sure
why the giant reptiles disappeared.
Only their bones and their tracks in rocks
tell us where they lived,
long ago in the day of the dinosaurs.